AMBULANCES

by Michelle Levine

Pull Ahead Books

Lerner Publications Company • Minneapolis

This book is available in two editions:
Library binding by Lerner Publications Company, a division of Lerner Publishing Group
Soft cover by First Avenue Editions, an imprint of Lerner Publishing Group
241 First Avenue North
Minneapolis, MN 55401 U.S.A.

Website address: www.lernerbooks.com

Library of Congress Cataloging-in-Publication Data

Michelle Levine.
        Ambulances / By Michelle Levine.
            p.   cm. – (Pull ahead books)
        Summary: Simple text describes how ambulances rush
    to emergencies to take hurt or sick people to the hospital,
    including how the lights and siren operate and where the
    emergency medical technicians store their equipment.
        ISBN: 0–8225–0769–2 (lib. bdg. : alk. paper)
        ISBN: 0–8225–9923–6 (pbk. : alk. paper)
        1. Ambulances–Juvenile literature. [1. Ambulances.]
    I. Title. II. Series.
    TL235.8.W38 2004
    362.18'8–dc22   2003012848

Manufactured in the United States of America
1 2 3 4 5 6 – JR – 09 08 07 06 05 04

Move over, cars! Something speedy is on the road. What is it?

This is an ambulance.   Ambulances
rush to **emergencies.** They take sick
or hurt people to the hospital.

This ambulance is in a hurry.

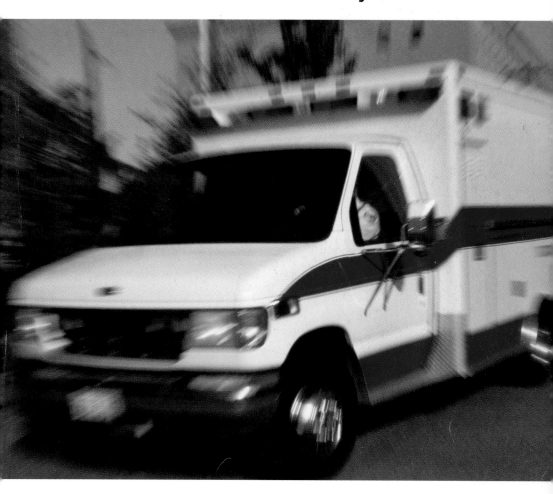

Bright lights flash.

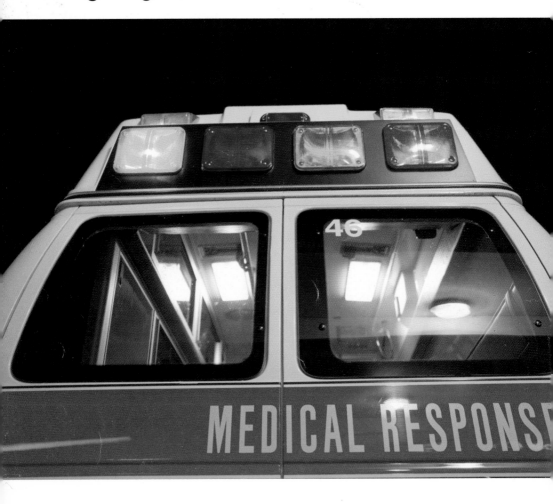

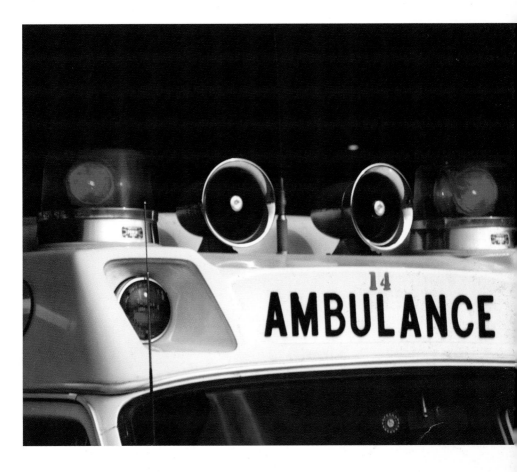

Loud **sirens** howl. WHEE-OOO!
What are the lights and sirens for?

The lights and sirens warn drivers that an ambulance is coming. Cars must pull over to let it by.

Four wheels take the ambulance to an emergency. An **engine** gives the wheels power.

The front of the ambulance is where the driver sits.

Inside, the driver pushes buttons. The buttons turn the ambulance's lights and sirens on or off.

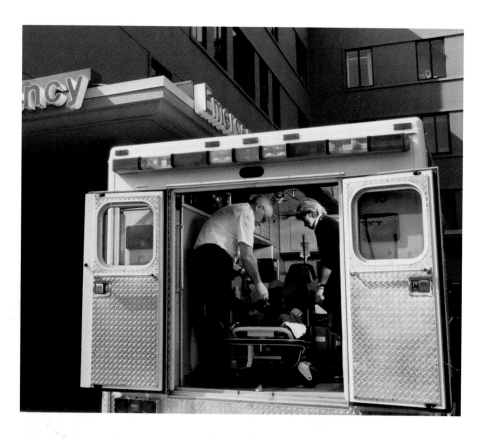

EMTs ride in the back of the
ambulance. EMTs are Emergency
Medical Technicians.

EMTs use special **equipment** to help sick or hurt people. Where do EMTs keep their equipment?

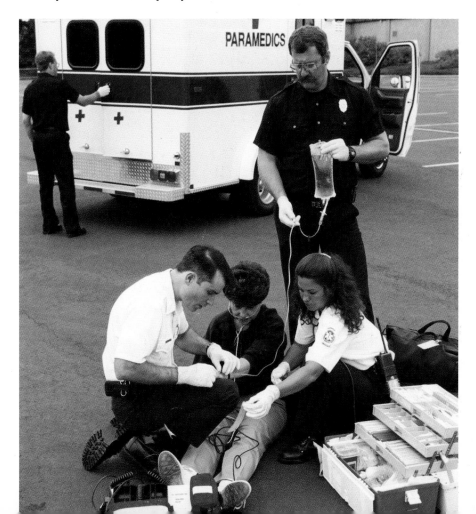

Many **cabinets** are in back of the ambulance.

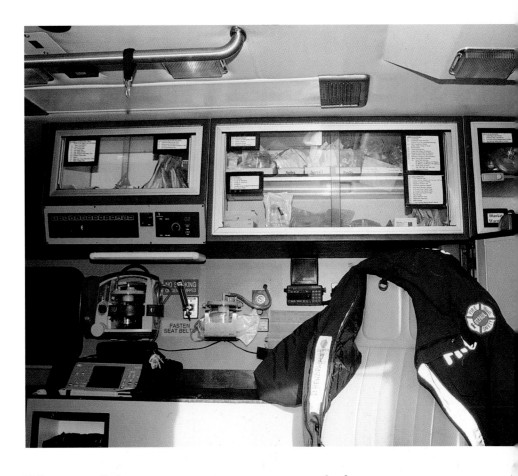

The cabinets store some of the equipment for EMTs

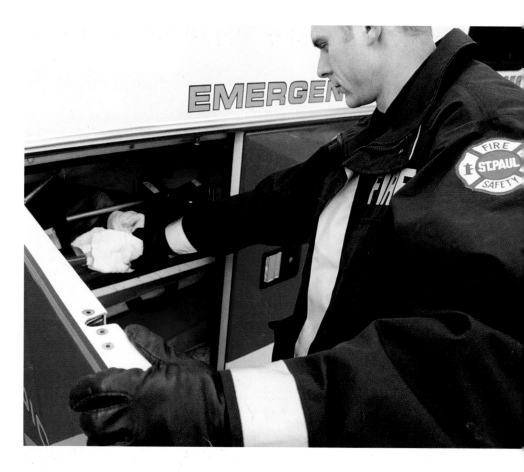

Doors on the outside of the ambulance open up.

More equipment is stored behind them.

This ambulance has arrived at an emergency.

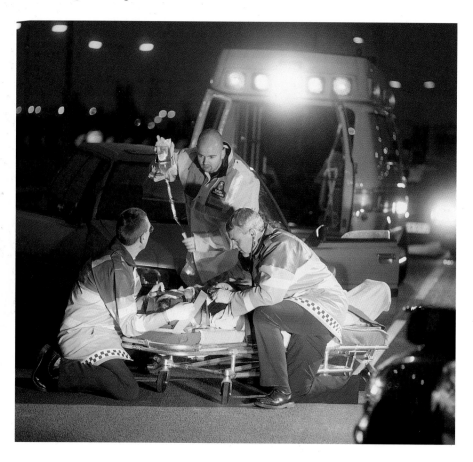

EMTs carry the **patient** into the back of the ambulance. Wide doors let the patient through.

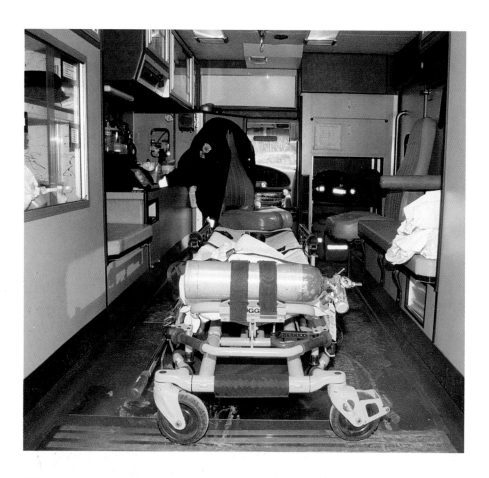

The back of the ambulance has room
for the patient and the EMTs.

EMTs sit near the patient on chairs and benches. They take care of the patient on the way to the hospital.

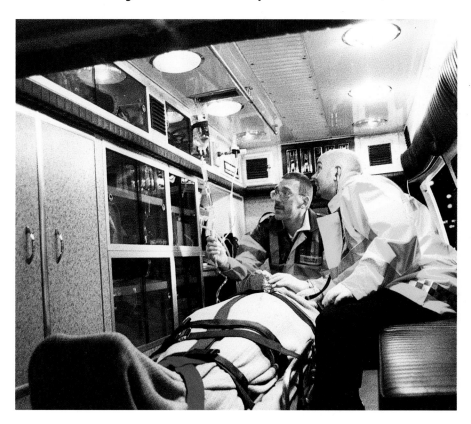

This ambulance has arrived at a hospital. What happens next?

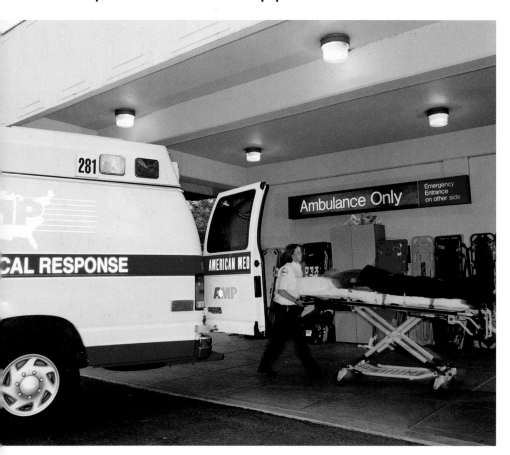

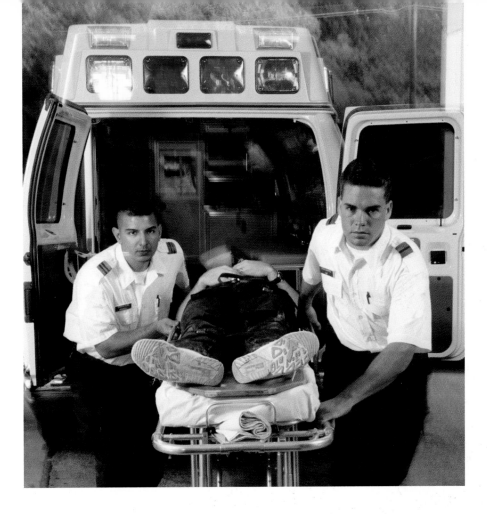

EMTs rush the patient inside. The ambulance's work is done.

This ambulance is on its way home.

Some ambulances stay at hospitals. Other ambulances belong to fire departments or police stations.

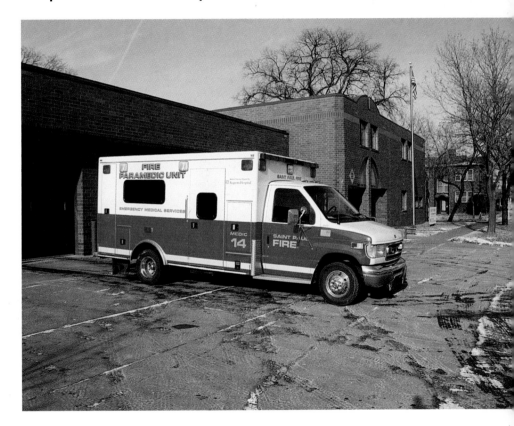

But all ambulances do the same job.

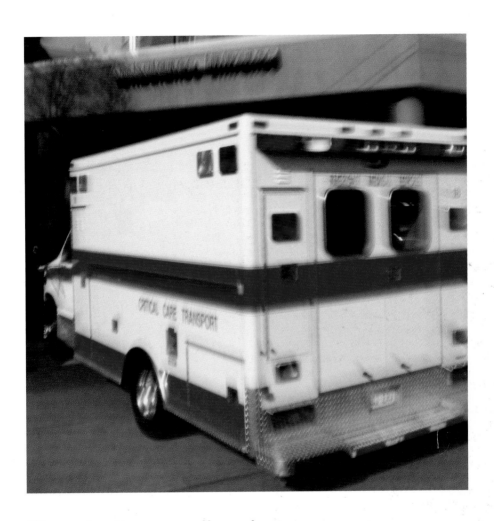

They help save lives!

Fun Facts about Ambulances

- Most ambulances are either vans or trucks that are specially made to do their job.

- Sometimes airplanes and helicopters are used as ambulances. Airplanes can travel much more quickly than trucks. And helicopters can get to places that cars cannot.

- The first ambulances were used in Europe more than 500 years ago. These ambulances were wagons pulled by horses. They helped rescue soldiers who were hurt during a war.

- Most ambulances have a telephone in the back of the ambulance. That way, EMTs can talk to doctors and nurses on the way to the hospital.

Parts of an Ambulance

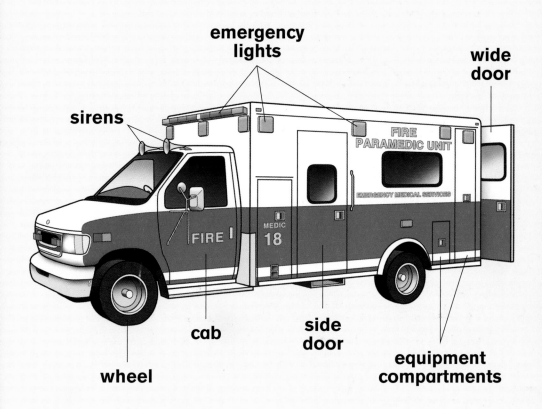

emergency lights

wide door

sirens

cab

wheel

side door

equipment compartments

Glossary

cabinets: places that store things. Most cabinets have shelves and doors.

emergencies: serious problems that need help quickly

EMTs: Emergency Medical Technicians. EMTs help sick or hurt people in emergencies.

engine: the part of an ambulance that gives it the power to move

equipment: tools used to help sick or hurt people

patient: a person who is sick or hurt and needs to go to the hospital

sirens: the parts of ambulances that make loud warning sounds

Index

About the Author

Michelle Levine is a writer and editor living in St. Paul, Minnesota.

Photo Acknowledgments

The photographs in this book appear courtesy of: © Todd Strand/IPS, front cover, pp. 3, 4, 9, 10, 11, 15, 16, 17, 20, 24, 25, 31; © PhotoDisc Royalty Free by Getty Images, pp. 5, 6, 7, 8, 12, 13, 14, 18, 19, 21, 22, 23, 26, 27.